Get You in 30 Days or Less!

- The Complete Step By Step Plan to Get Your Ex Back for Good! •

By Eric Monroe

www.Eric-Monroe.com

Copyright © 2016. All rights reserved. This book may not be reproduced in any form, in whole or in part without written permission from the author.

Table of Contents

Don't Worry – Time to Be Happy 4

Why Did You Break Up? 9

Step 1: Go Radio Silent 16

Step 2: Time to Heal 23

Step 3: Step Up Your Game 28

Step 4: Handle Other People 36

Step 5: Turn the Tables 40

Step 6: Start Dating 44

Step 7: Start Broadcasting Your New Life 48

Step 8: Take a Reality Check 52

Step 9: Be Elusive 55

Step 10: Play on His Mind 60

Step 10: Avoid His Bait at All Costs! 64

Step 11: Have THAT Conversation 67

What Happens if He's With Someone Else? 72

A Final Word: Building a Better, Stronger Future With Your Ex 75

Don't Worry – Time to Be Happy

If you're reading these words, it's because you are right at this moment going through one of the worst experiences it's possible for a person to have. You've just broken up with your ex boyfriend and you're currently grieving the loss of a huge part of your life, the main focus of your heart and something you thought was going to last for the rest of your lives together.

I'm so sorry – I really am. I know how badly you're hurting right now and just how miserable, helpless and lost a break up makes you feel. I know what a huge hole this has blasted right through your heart.

But I also have good news: it doesn't have to stay this way. I've written this book and packed it with all my experience and knowledge to help you show your ex boyfriend that he's made a terrible mistake.

I've written this foolproof guide not only to help you salvage something special, but to make sure you go about it the right way. Why? Because what your heart is telling you to do at this very moment is almost certainly exactly the wrong thing.

You need to avoid doing that wrong thing, and for that you need my help as an objective, outside expert. You need someone who understands the male psyche and knows what is needed if you're going to remind him what he's missing and get this relationship back together.

You need someone to tell you what mistakes you're about to make and why they're not going to work. You need someone who understands what your automatic natural reactions are going to be and can help you turn those into something much more positive.

This method has been proven to work countless times, so you can feel confident that you're in safe hands. I am a relationship expert and break ups come with the territory – I've walked so many of my clients through this heartbreaking time and I've helped dozens of them reignite the romance and win back their exes.

A break up doesn't have to be the end, if it's handled right – but the sad thing is that it usually isn't. And just to show you exactly how well I empathize with what's running through your mind right now, let me take some guesses as to what you've been planning to do about it.

You want to text him, to let him know you're sorry or convince him to come back or to share your distress and anguish in the hopes it will change his mind. You want to call him, over and over, especially late at night when you're feeling lonely and vulnerable or when you've had a drink or two and it's lowered your defenses even though you normally know it's the wrong thing to do.

You have no idea how to function like a normal human being right now. You can barely clamber out of bed in the morning, let alone be a productive member of society. You don't want to eat, you aren't sleeping well, you wake up with tears in your eyes.

You don't understand how things went so wrong and you just know you could fix them if he gave you a chance. You're almost certainly right, but you don't know how to convince him of that.

You want to try "accidentally" turning up some place where you know he's going to be, you're even considering just appearing on his doorstep. You want to plead with him until he changes his mind, show him just how good the two of you were together and how silly he is to want to walk away.

You might be considering even more sneaky approaches – sending him messages and then claiming they were supposed to be for someone else, just to get him to respond, or calling him for "another reason", like to cheerily let him know the electricity bill just came in before you "subtly" turn the conversation to getting back together.

You think maybe if you make him jealous he'll realize how much he loves you and you've been stalking his Facebook profile every five minutes for some small sign that he still cares.

All of these things are the wrong way to get your ex back. Doing any single one of them is going to do a lot more damage than it does any good.

I know, and I do understand, that it seems like it's flat out impossible to sit on your hands and wait around – you need to be doing *something*, or doesn't it mean that you've accepted the romance is dead?

I'm going to help you dispel that thinking and understand that doing nothing is sometimes doing everything. I'm going to give you some guaranteed steps to follow – and I'm going to make sure you understand why they work.

Keep this book with you from now until you get that ex back in your arms, where he's supposed to do. Make it your religion.

Right here and right now, we're going to start a journey together. By the end of it, you will have your ex back in your life, you'll be a happier and more positive person and you'll feel confident that your relationship is ready to stand the test of time.

So take my hand and let's start those steps right now. I'll be with you every step of the way.

Why Did You Break Up?

No break-up ever came completely out of the blue. Anyone who tells you that everything seemed absolutely fine right up until the moment that the romance ended is almost certainly either lying or totally delusional.

So, while it might be a tough thing to do right now, we're going to need to figure out exactly why he ended things. It's important for two reasons. First, it will help you decide whether he's really worth bringing back into your life, because you're guaranteed to make that happen if you continue on through this book.

Second, it will give you a clearer idea of how to proceed and tailor the advice I'm about to give you for your own needs. You'll know whose fault it is that things have come to this point (yes, it is someone's fault, even if that's hard to hear, and yes, usually it's both parties' faults, even when one of you performed the final act of betrayal that brought things crashing to an end) and how to make amends.

There are a lot of reasons for a relationship falling apart and it's impossible to identify them all, but there are also a few common categories that the vast majority fall into.

1. **One of you cheated.** This one is tricky because it can either be the actual reason for the breakup or a symptom of something else. A lot of people cheat because something big and important is missing from their relationship and their emotional needs force them to seek it elsewhere. Maybe one of you wasn't being affectionate enough, or maybe one of you didn't feel appreciated. On the other hand, some guys – and girls – cheat because it's in their nature. If you're dealing with the latter category, I'd suggest thinking carefully before you decide to get him back. If he cheated once, he's likely to cheat again. If he found comfort with someone else because things between you were going wrong, on the other hand, there is arguably more reason to forgive him and move on.

2. **He got bored.** Human beings thrive on change and have a serious problem with stagnation. If he felt like the relationship was getting boring and there was nothing to look forward to or feel excited about, you can hardly blame him

for wanting to find what he needs elsewhere. But don't worry – we're going to fix that problem.

3. **He felt like you took him for granted.** This one is a little bit similar to getting bored – both problems stem from the relationship stagnating over time. At first, you may have displayed the heady flushes of excitement whenever he brought you a gift or did something special just to please you. It's natural to stop feeling quite the same level of joy after time passes – but it's also not a good thing. He will naturally and understandably start to wonder why he bothers.

4. **One of you changed.** Life happens, there's no getting away from that. Maybe one of you lost a job and took a hit to your confidence and happiness levels. Maybe there was a death in the family, or simply a change that made day to day life get busier and harder. It's not something that can never be fixed, it's just going to mean recognizing and addressing that problem.

5. **You got co-dependent.** Some romances get hot and heavy fast and the two of you quite literally can't get enough of each other. You become co-dependent and both of you begin to change just to facilitate that. At first, it's a wonderful feeling. But then, one of you will come to the realization that you're not the same people you were when you met and you're maybe a little worse off for that fact. Again, this can be fixed: you can still be in love without needing to breathe within the same oxygen bubble 24 hours of each day.

6. **Issues in your lives are causing conflict.** Maybe it's a case of different views on marriage or parenthood, or a difference in religion or background, maybe you just have completely different ideas as to where you want to hang out in the evening. These things don't have to be deal breakers, but they can seem that way in the moment. If one of you wants to travel the world and the other wants to further their career, or if one of you wants to stay in your home town and the other wants to move to the big city, it's not uncommon for one party to decide things can never work. That's not true, though making them work is going to

require dedication and active input from both of you.

7. **Too much negativity.** A relationship that's turned bad is a lot like the old legend of the snake that swallowed its own tail. Something small niggles one of you, causing small rifts and arguments that create larger niggles, which in turn lead to bigger rifts. The more it goes on, the more negativity there is and the harder it becomes to remember what was so good about the relationship in the first place. It makes sense to end things at that point on an emotional level, but on an objective level there are few niggles that cannot be fixed with some honest communication and effort.

8. **Outside influences.** There's a reason we make jokes about mothers-in-law: it's because they can pose a genuine threat to even the most stable partnership if they disapprove of it even happening. The same goes for other family members and even close friends. If they make a genuine effort to destabilize the two of you, it can be problematic because their opinions and needs count highly – of course they do. But don't be fooled into thinking this cannot be

overcome – like anything else, it's just going to take work.

9. **He acted badly – or you did.** Everyone makes mistakes, because we're all human – but all of us also have issues that we simply cannot ignore or forgive. If you've done something he's finding it hard to get past, there is still hope – but you'll have to work extra hard to get to that point.

10. **The romance just faded away.** Sometimes there's no big and obvious smoking gun when a relationship dies. Instead, it's a culmination of smaller things, usually covered in the points above, that add up to a partnership no longer working. It feels like that is going to have to be the end, but it doesn't need to be. The same rules apply: effort and determination will win the day.

So which of these categories do you fall into, or which one comes closest to your situation?

One thing is for sure: if he's the one who ended it, then it's a sure bet you weren't ready for it to be over. You still had hope that things would work out and the two of you could have your very own fairytale happy ending.

If he ended it, he's the one who lost hope – and we're going to give that hope back to him. So let's get started, shall we?

Step 1: Go Radio Silent

Of all the advice I'm going to give you in this book, I can tell you right now that you'll find this piece the hardest to follow. You're going to have to use every last strand of willpower you have, so brace yourself.

You're going to go radio silent. I mean it – no contact with your ex at all. Even if every fiber of your being wants to ask him what went wrong or tell him that you're really, really sorry, you need to do whatever it takes to resist that urge.

I know, I know: it seems counterproductive, at best, and like a death knell to your chances at worst. If you don't call him or send him a message, how is he going to know that you want him back?

The first and most important reason that this simply isn't going to work is that you're not in a good place right now to make things better. The end of a relationship that held an important position in your heart and in your life is no different to a death in its impact on your emotions – sometimes even on your health.

You are grieving, and that brings with it all the different and painful stages of grief. You're hurt and angry, distressed and lonely, helpless and depressed, and all those things are swimming around in your head. You need to heal yourself before you'll ever have a hope of healing the damage.

What you will naturally want to do at this moment is handle the shock of things ending by getting all of the facts and feelings out into the open. I understand that compulsion, but you have work to do before reconnecting with your ex and it's far more important right now that you work on yourself.

Think of this stage as the healing process for you. By going radio silent, you're going to give yourself the time you need to recover and then move on. You're equipping yourself to take a real shot at getting your ex back – and I promise you that you'll have a lot more luck when you do try.

It's not the only reason to go radio silent, either. Despite how much it's going to hurt, it's also the most powerful tool in your arsenal at this very moment. Why? For many different reasons:

- A period of no contact gives you time to calm down and recover from all the negative emotions you're feeling, and it does the same thing for him. If he's angry with you or feeling betrayed and hurt, he will have time to process those raw emotions before you start suggesting any positive steps forward. Think about the last time you were hopping mad with a friend or member of your family: if they'd come to you with the solution right away, would you have accepted it with open arms or told them to go stick it up their proverbials? Likely the latter, and that's how he'll be feeling too. Now is just not the right time to try.

- You're going to fall apart, go to pieces and melt into puddles for a little while after the breakup. That's natural and to be expected, but it's also a terrible mindset from which to try to mend things. You cannot and should not be expected to keep your cool and act rationally. Until you can control your feelings and keep your emotions in check, you have no business trying to make sensible decisions. Allow yourself this time – find a good friend, a sibling or even a helpline to get you through it. Wait until you're less emotional before you start putting your game plan in place.

- If you call your ex every half an hour to tell him how much you miss him and pen long missives on your chat app explaining why your relationship was the romance of the century, he knows exactly what you're thinking. And, let's face it, what you're thinking is nothing good – it's tiring, especially if he's angry, and it's going to make him want you to stop talking and disappear. On the other hand, if you've gone radio silent, he has no idea what's going on in your head. Do you miss him? Are you upset? Are you already out partying with other guys? Men love a mystery and they cannot resist a challenge. Radio silence puts him in the perfect frame of mind for reconciliation simply by turning you from an ex to be avoided into a challenge he wants to pursue. That's going to take some time, but this is the first step to that outcome.

- Unless you were in the type of relationship that is entirely based around passionate, high octane fighting matches (and, if you were, it might be time to reconsider rekindling that particular flame), your man probably doesn't appreciate dramatics. Men don't really understand the extreme emotions that you're going through right now – ever noticed that blank look that passes over his face when you cry? And because he doesn't understand it, his first reaction is to avoid it. By showing him how you're feeling, you will be pushing him further away because he will come to think of you as a drama queen rather than a woman of character to be respected. It's unfair, but it's true.

- Radio silence makes you unavailable – especially if he is trying to contact you and you're not responding. Men want what they cannot immediately have, which instantly makes you more attractive to him. When he knows he can have you back in an instant, he doesn't need to try, which means you're not interesting or much of a conquest.

- If he ended the relationship, he's the one who rejected you. By going radio silent and not answering any communications he sends your way, you are effectively rejecting him in return. That's going to lead to him feeling a lot less like the one in control and a lot more like you're holding all the cards. And from there, it's entirely possible he's going to be the one begging YOU to change your mind. Again, that's going to happen a little way down the road, but don't worry: we're going to get there.

- When you're not there, your ex has the chance to miss you. You won't be there to laugh when something makes him think of one of your inside jokes, you won't be around when he goes to your favorite restaurant, the house will be quiet and lonely when he gets home in the evenings. These are the parts of your relationship he took for granted, and they will start to leave a big and painful hole in his life.

As I think you can clearly see by now, radio silence has a myriad of benefits and not many disadvantages. The only significant downside is how it's going to make you feel and just how much effort you'll need to put in to resisting that temptation.

So have a sleepover with your best friend and talk it through till you both fall asleep as the dawn starts to break. Go out with a group of good pals and party till dawn to take your mind off it – but make sure they have your phone in case a little drinking gets through your willpower. Spend a few evenings watching sad movies and eating ice cream. Cry, floods of tears that seem like they're never going to stop.

Do whatever you need to do right now – let those emotions flow. Just, whatever you do, don't let him see them flowing.

As a side note: there's no need to actually let him, or anyone else, know that you're planning to go radio silent. Let him wonder whether you're doing it on purpose and avoid the dramatics of making a big statement or announcement.

Simply go radio silent in absolutely every form of communication that's available to you. No calling him on the phone, no emailing him, no "accidentally" turning up at his favorite bar, not even an apology for whatever you think you've done wrong.

From this moment on, he is not going to hear a single peep from you. And rest assured that he is going to wonder why.

Step 2: Time to Heal

Once you've purged all those hurtful emotions and you're all cried out, it's time to go back to the list in the first chapter of this book and work out exactly what brought you to this breakup in the first place. Be honest with yourself: is it your fault, or at least partly to do with something you said or did?

Honesty is vital here, no matter how much it hurts. Unless we own up to our mistakes, there's not much we can do to fix them.

It's going to be tough to accept that there are probably a lot of different reasons why you broke up. Take a long, hard look at the evidence with clear eyes and a clear mind. Think back to the times when you argued, when one of you clearly wasn't happy or when a red flag went up that things were not quite as good as you thought they should be. What is that evidence telling you? Which categories apply to your situation?

Our aim here is to reset your emotions. Whatever led you to this point, you need to go back to being the woman he courted and fell in love with in the first place. This isn't just for him, either – if the two of you have broken up, it means there were problems, and even if he's the hurting party then you'll still be showing some scars. You're wounded, and now is the time to get you back up to full emotional health.

It is a little bit for him, of course. We can admit that just between you and me.

Well, maybe more than a little bit. For whatever reasons, something about you has changed, so we want to remind him of the independent, lively, loveable person you were when he first met you and decided he wanted to make you his woman.

So let's follow a few steps to get you rejuvenated and back on track, ready to show your ex exactly what he's missing out on:

- For a little while at least, it's time to crawl into your comfort zone. It doesn't really matter exactly what that is – it's different for everyone. Maybe working out helps get your mind off things, maybe watching endless old movies or reading books or spending time with your faithful pet is the key. Maybe it's your religion, your relationship with a close friend or even your work. Whatever brings you comfort, indulge yourself. It's going to take a while before the urge to burst into tears fades away when certain songs come on the radio and you don't have a lump in your throat from the moment you wake up in the morning. Understand that it's absolutely fine and normal to feel this way and you shouldn't feel guilty or ashamed if life can't quite continue as usual. Be kind to yourself: give yourself the comfort you need to feel better.

- As soon as you feel able, change up your routine as much as is reasonably possible. It's going to be the little things that break you for a while: running across pictures of the two of you together, walking to work along the route that the two of you once took together, the s'more ingredients that you always used on snow days when you were both stuck in the house with nowhere to go. Get rid of all the memories that make you miss him the most: clear our your social media photo folders, file away his emails, hide the mementos you have around the house. You're not doing this forever, you're just taking him out of the equation for a little while until you are healed.

- Reward yourself for your progress. You're still in a period of radio silence, so treat yourself to something that makes you feel good every time you manage to make it through a certain amount of time without sending him a single text. Again, this goes back to your comfort zone: do whatever makes you happy and don't be afraid to indulge. Rewarding yourself helps you to solidify in your own mind that what you're doing is definitely the right thing.

- Do the things that made you happy before the relationship. You were already a whole person before your ex came along – a person who was amazing enough to attract him. Maybe you stopped doing those things, maybe they morphed into something you did together, maybe you carried on with them but not quite as much. Start spending some proper, dedicated time doing them again, whether it's hiking at the weekends or cooking wonderful dinners for your friends.

- Pamper yourself. There's nothing like putting on clothes you feel great in, doing your make up nicely, visiting a spa for the day and getting a makeover to help you feel more like yourself again. You might feel broken on the inside, but trust me that it will help you feel better if you look more like yourself on the outside.

Your job right now is to remind yourself of the woman you really are and all those wonderful things about yourself that you were known for pre-ex boyfriend. For a while, it's going to be tough, and that's to be expected. But, as time goes by, you'll find it gets easier and easier.

I know it doesn't feel as though that's true right now, but that's because you're in one of the stages of grieving. You're mourning the loss of something that made up a huge part of your life and it's just fine to take your time to do that.

As soon as you feel ready, start to take those small steps towards being whole again. And, remember, not a peep to your ex all the time that you are working on your healing!

Step 3: Step Up Your Game

At this point in the process, you will begin to feel more objective about the situation. Your thoughts on whether you want to get back together with your ex, what needs to change if you do and how to go about it will begin to evolve.

Pretty soon here, we're going to initiate a foolproof plan to get him back in your arms for good. But before we do that, there's another important step you'll want to take.

It's time to improve yourself. When he sees you again, you want to not only be the woman he fell in love with, but someone more irresistible still. I mean that on several different levels: you want to be even more interesting and enticing, you want to have solved whatever issues to do with your own behavior that you have identified as keeping the two of you apart and you want to be bursting with the kind of confidence and self worth he will have no idea how to resist.

A break up has some horrible side effects above and beyond the grief and the disruption to your lifestyle. When the man you were in love with rejects you, it's a blow to your ego and self esteem like very few others. It's hard to come back from that, especially in a situation where you might not be entirely sure what caused it to happen.

Not to mention the embarrassment at having "failed". All your friends and family knew you were in a relationship and how happy the two of you were together, yet here you are apart seemingly for good. A part of you can't help but feel as though people are judging you for that failure.

The reality, of course, is that you are not a failure. Even if the end of the romance was entirely your mistake, you are still not a failure. Life happens, we're all human: this was an event, not a description of who you are as a person.

Confidence is something that only exists when you have the self esteem to underpin it. You cannot exude the kind of confident aura that has people flocking to your side if you don't genuinely believe you are a person worth flocking to.

It's also one of the hardest things to maintain, because there's so much about life, society and the world that seems hell bent on knocking us off our own pedestals. Right now, and into the future, you're going to have to win that battle against the things that tell you you're not worth it.

I'm going to share some tips for building your self esteem that right now you might not see the value in taking. That's because you're right at the bottom of the self esteem barrel in the days and months after a break up, so you will automatically reject any idea of building back up again.

Yes, it's going to be hard and, no, you're not going to enjoy every last minute of it. But if you want to get your ex back, you need to look him in the eye knowing that you're worth coming back to.

- Make a list of every positive attribute about yourself you can think of. I want you to make this an ongoing process, which isn't going to be difficult because the list could go on forever. I'm not just talking about the big stuff, like "won a scholarship to school" or "got a big promotion". I'm talking about everything down to the tiniest traits – the fact that you always give up your seat on the bus for the elderly, that time you made dinner for a neighbor's family because they were going through a hard time, the little dimple in your chin. Because you're doubting yourself right now, your mind is automatically picking up on every single flaw it can find, throwing those things at you endlessly to remind you how worthless you really are. It's one hell of a skewed picture, because it leaves out all the good things. Nobody's perfect, of course you have faults, but that's not ALL of who you are. Maybe you do have a habit of dropping your laundry next to the basket instead of putting it inside, but you also volunteered to help plant a community garden and you make a mean apple pie. We want to turn your mind around and start it thinking about the good side of you. So start that list now, keep it handy and add to it whenever you think of something new – after a while, it will help to turn the flow of your thoughts.

- Forgive yourself for the bad, stupid and ill advised things you've done. If you left your father's good fishing equipment out in the rain and it rusted, what does that matter now? If you betrayed a friend's confidence one time and she was mad at you, make sure you've asked for her forgiveness and then let go of it. If you got drunk at the office party and did something embarrassing, tell yourself you won't make that mistake again and then forget about it. It does you no good to hold on to these things. They are life lessons, so learn the lesson and move on.

- Go back to your list of good qualities and mark off the ones that make you particularly proud. Turn them into statements, such as, "I'm kind to every stranger and I'm great at making people feel comfortable," or, "I've done right by my friends and family and I look great in a short skirt". When you catch yourself doubting something about who you are, what you look like or the things you do, repeat these to yourself – over and over, until you've actually heard your own words.

- Reward yourself for the good things you do. I know, you don't perform acts of kindness and charity for the reward and you don't build your own character just so you can buy a new pair of shoes. I'm talking about making yourself a whiteboard sign with smiley faces every time you feel proud of yourself, or a pot of your favorite candy you can eat only when you feel positive. It's not really a reward, as rewards traditionally go. It's a way to continually remind yourself of how many good, admirable and worthy things you say, do and think on a daily basis. Just in case you forget.

- If there are things you don't like about yourself, change them. There's no point beating yourself up because you hate your haircut – get a new one. Don't wallow in misery because you can't seem to get to work on time – make a change so you arrive a few minutes earlier. We all have a tendency to concentrate on the bad and convince ourselves we are powerless to change it, but that's not true. Change is entirely in your own hands.

- Write down your bucket list. I don't care if you're 18 years old and you have a lifetime to get them done – now's the time to identify all those dreams and exciting things you wanted to try. You'll end up with a long list by the time you're done (if you haven't, stop feeling sorry for yourself for a moment, get back to that list and keep adding). Now pick around 10 to 15 of them and write them down together. These are the things you're going to try. For now, choose just three of them and get going on them immediately. Doing something brand new won't just keep your mind off your ex, it will also bring a whole new level of enjoyment into your life that will improve your morale and your self esteem at the same time. Not only that, you also become more interesting when you have lots of things going on in your life, and that's going to intrigue and entice your ex.

- In the process, watch for every opportunity to expand and diversify your social group. Make new friends and acquaintances and take advantage of those brand new relationships to try even more new things together. These people do not know you in the context of your past – they are not privy to your break up. You don't need to wallow in those emotions with them, you can be a version of yourself who is free to make the most out of life. The same rule applies: you will be adding new and interesting things to your play book that in turn make you a fascinating person in your ex's eyes.

It's a slow road from broken and defeated to confident and proud, but you'll be glad you decided to take it. This part is for you, not for him, and you'll need to be absolutely genuine in your desire to improve if you're planning to make real change.

It's also a big part of your game plan to win back your ex – it's just that winning him back cannot be the sole reason for your efforts. He'll be able to tell the difference between real, positive improvements and a facade that's meant to impress him, trust me.

Walk that road, and walk it proud. When you reach the end, and your ex is standing in front of you, just imagine how irresistible he's going to find this very best version of you.

Step 4: Handle Other People

Break ups don't take place in a vacuum. There are always other people watching you and, while it really isn't true that they're going to think you're a failure, it can still be a pain in the butt to have to handle their attention.

This is especially true in the ultra connected modern world. Where once upon a time we might have been whispered about at the garden gates throughout the village, now we have hundreds of people watching us through the glare of the internet. Old friends and workmates, people we knew at school, that random guy you met in a bar while you were on vacation in the Bahamas. We collect all of them on Facebook and then tell them everything intimate about our lives.

Even the most conservative of us will have at least mentioned our relationships in public once or twice, and heavy social media users will likely have done so a whole lot more. Again, it's natural – your ex was a big part of your life and so you include him in your updates.

We've all seen the messy fallouts where scorned women begin berating their exes on social media, announcing how awful they are, leaving cryptic messages in the form of song lyrics and posting pictures of themselves draped over another guy.

I'm telling you right now: do NOT do that. You need to delete your ex's profile from social media and any of his close friends and family if you think you will give in to the temptation to make statements of that ilk for their benefit (or that you might drunk-message them at 1 a.m. pleading for their help in getting him back).

Don't air your dirty laundry in this very public place. Avoid it altogether during those painful first stages, then try to concentrate only on the positive when you're on the road to recovery.

Instead, you need to focus on two sets of people. First, the people who are genuinely affected by this break up. Second, the people you can rely on to stand by your side as you work through it.

Nobody else needs to know a thing about it. Great Aunt Flo would prefer to see you post a cake recipe and that bitchy girl from the downstairs office does not need fodder for her snark. When and if you decide to change your relationship status, do it in such a way that it isn't broadcast all over people's news feeds. This is private to you: you don't want to make a huge drama of it, both for your own sake and because you can bet your bottom dollar that all that emotional fallout will make its way back to his ears. And, as we've mentioned, he's really not interested in drama and histrionics.

Moving on to the people you *should* be talking to, the second group is going to be the most important at first. Reach out to your loved ones as soon as you can and ask them for their support. That's what we have loved ones for, after all. Let them be there to support you, whether that means crying all night on the phone with you or making sure you're stocked up on ice cream and chocolates.

If the two of you were heavily involved with one another's social groups or families, wait a little while until you are feeling less emotional before you reach out to them. Make sure that those people who are concerned it will affect their own relationship with you have been reassured you will handle this with dignity and respect.

Make sure anyone who will be affected practically is also kept up to date. If, for instance, you planned a double date vacation with your friends and you're far from likely to be going with them now, let them know you haven't forgotten them and that you have a plan to solve the issue.

Deal with other people at this time with as much dignity as you can muster. You may regret lashing out at them or bearing your soul for the world to see, but you will never regret dealing with people in a respectful, positive manner – and their opinion of you can only improve further.

Not to mention that, once again, a certain someone is bound to catch wind of how well you've been handling things, and taking the high road will be a big positive tick in the right box when it's time to coax him back into your life.

Step 5: Turn the Tables

Around a week after the break up first happens is your one and only opportunity to break that radio silence. It's a cunning little trick that's going to have a far bigger effect on what he's thinking than you'd ever suspect.

Let me stress again that you absolutely should not do this right away – you need to wait at least a week. If you're still feeling too emotional to handle it at that point, you can always ask a friend for their help in composing your words.

You're going to send him one message that makes it clear the relationship is over.

You might be wondering what the point of that is when he's already kicked you to the curb. You both already know it's over, right?

Actually, no. The break up conversation is just the first step of the actual process and he will subconsciously be waiting for the next one. Usually there will be endless conversations, pleading messages and traumatic arguments before both parties are ready to accept things are definitely over.

You're going to leap frog over all those in between moments and go straight in for the kill. You won't see the effects of this immediately – it will take a while for this ripple to finally reach the edges of the pond. But, trust me, by the time we've finished playing out this game plan, you'll definitely be seeing the effects.

Write him a very brief message that includes just a few lines and covers the following:

- Your desire to formally end things and bring closure to the relationship.
- A parting statement about how much you will miss a particularly poignant part of your shared lives together.
- A simple goodbye.

Keep it simple, keep it brief and keep it positive. Resist any urges you may feel to apologize for what happened, throw any blame at him, explain yourself or touch on the break up in any way at all.

All you are doing in this letter is saying goodbye for good. Or, at least, that's all he will think you are doing.

Send that letter and then move on to the next step of your game plan. In the meantime, here's what will be going on at the other end:

In the days after the break up, he was angry and emotional and assumed you were feeling the same way. If he ended it, he assumed you would soon be turning up on his doorstep begging him to come back and playing your special song on a portable boom box. He was expecting apologies and recriminations – and that's not what he got.

Your letter will stop him in his tracks and make him question the accepted flow of the break up. He will be thrown by this and will not know what to make of your words.

He will not be able to find any fault with what you have said – you were reasonable and seemingly doing exactly what he wanted you to do. But it won't feel right.

Instead, you've turned the tables on him and become the one who finally said goodbye – you took the power out of his hands completely. Now he's the one who has been rejected, not you.

Even more importantly, your message was almost entirely positive. You said goodbye without any hint of blame, begging or emotion. You remembered a happy moment and implied that you will continue to remember it and hold it in your heart.

He didn't get the backlash he was dreading, instead he got a message that ended with a simple, "goodbye". It will throw him, confuse him and, most importantly of all, make him sad.

Over time, this feeling will continue to grow, even if he was too livid with you when he first read it to really acknowledge his reaction. He'll start feeling more positively towards you, he'll miss you and wonder what you're up to and he'll ponder the idea of getting back together. In one simple letter, you've turned the tables completely. You've helped him let go of a significant proportion of what caused the two of you to break up in the first place – and you've started him down the road of thinking about getting back together.

Step 6: Start Dating

I know exactly how you just reacted to the title of this chapter. Your eyebrows shot upward in your head, maybe there was a sharp intake of breath – there was definitely an instant negative reaction to the idea.

Why would you want to start dating? That's what you're asking me right now, I'm pretty sure of it. You know that you want your ex boyfriend back and you absolutely don't want anyone else, so why in the name of all things holy would you want to date another guy?

Let me explain why you need to do this.

- **It's a self confidence exercise.** By dating other men, you remind yourself that other men want to date you. You remind yourself that you are attractive and loveable and you deserve to have guys falling over themselves to spend time in your company.

- **It moves you to a different stage in your thinking.** Up until this moment, you have been thinking of yourself as His Ex Girlfriend. It's been all about him, every single step that you've taken up to this point, even when you've been working on yourself with a genuine goal of improvement. Dating other guys shifts you into a different gear: you accept that, right now, you are a single and independent woman and your life does not revolve around anyone else.

- **It keeps your options open.** You probably don't want to hear this, but there's a small chance you will end up not wanting to get back together with your ex after all. Once the healing is done and you've launched your life to a brand new level of amazing, you might look back and realize that the romance wasn't everything you thought it was at the time. If that happens, don't think that everything you've done so far was a waste of time. It helped you become whole again and get through a terrible time and it's helped you decide what your future should bring. It has still been the journey you need.

- **It will make him jealous.** No matter what happened to end the relationship, he still thinks of you as belonging to him. I'm not suggesting you should shout this from the rooftops, as that would only serve to make him think you're dating other men purely for his benefit. But if he does get wind of what you're doing, it's going to trigger some serious jealousy. There's nothing quite like the risk of another man getting to kiss you and put his hands on your naked skin to spark off his natural possessive instincts. You belong to him, and he will automatically feel rocked by this knowledge. He will have to acknowledge the fact that he might well be losing you, whereas until now he thought in the back of his mind that he was safe from that – you were still his if he decided he wanted you. Now he knows that he's not your only prospect and you'll become a conquest to him again – something he can't help but want to win back.

Sign yourself up for a few dating sites or hit up your friends for some suggestions on who might be a great guy to go on a date with. Get yourself back out there in the dating pool.

If you're rusty, don't worry – it's easy to pick up. You simply need to do a little research to find out where in your area is a great place to meet new people or what dating sites are popular in your region.

You may find it easier, at least at first, to go on dates with a few different guys rather than limit yourself to one. If there's a little niggle at the back of your mind that you're "cheating" on your ex, you can ease yourself into this step by spreading your time among four or five different guys.

You're not necessarily looking for the romance of a lifetime, though it's important that you remain open to the possibility. Not only because you might find someone more suitable than your ex, but because the whole experience will have a more powerful impact on your self esteem if you take it seriously.

Above all else, your goal is to have some fun. You're on an adventure. You're spending time with new people and having new experiences and all of this will enrich you in both the short and long term. Embrace this part of the journey – it's probably the most enjoyable one so far, if you allow it to be.

Show your ex boyfriend that he's not the only man in the world to have ever noticed you. More importantly, remind yourself that you are desirable and worth spending time and attention on – and not just if your ex boyfriend feels like granting you that privilege.

Step 7: Start Broadcasting Your New Life

Up until now, you've kept your recovery process largely to yourself and you've been subtle about the changes you've been making to your lifestyle. Now we're going to turn up the volume just a little bit so that we can be sure he'll catch wind of what you're doing.

Before we start, I just want to make one thing clear: it's important that you don't go over the top with this part of the process. Think about any of your friends or acquaintances who split up with a lover and then began shouting about how happy and content they were single/in their new relationship/back with a previous lover/swept up in a holiday romance.

Remember all those endless posts about how perfect everything about their lives was? Did they ring true for you, or did you suspect that your friend was mostly trying to catch the attention of a certain someone so as to either make them jealous or hurt them?

We don't want to do that. We don't want to give your ex boyfriend the slightest inkling that anything you're doing is for him, even though we both know that it is. And if we're going to achieve that, we're going to need to be very, very subtle indeed.

Even if you're still healing and you're feeling bitter and dejected, you don't want to let that show – but, on the other hand, you don't want to be overly happy, either. The goldilocks zone for this part of the process is "content": back to your normal self and conversing with people just as you always have done in the past, before the break up.

Combine that with the letter you sent your ex and he's going to be certain that you've moved on and no longer need him. And you can imagine just how he's going to react to that – it's going to spark a desire to win back your love, even if it's a spark that he can't quite put his finger on yet.

Should you interact with mutual friends, or even with his friends and family? Sure, if it's something you would usually do. You don't want to step too far outside your normal behavior and, remember, you don't want to show even overly positive emotions because he'll see straight through them.

Post a few pictures of your new hobbies – let your friends know what you've been up to. Be nonchalant about it, even if that new hobby is skydiving or saving orphans in the third world. It's perfectly normal to share your achievements with the people you care about, after all, but you need to avoid any indication that you're doing these things just to show him how amazing you are.

Should you mention that you're dating while you're doing this? Yes, but only if it comes up naturally. Don't post countless pictures of yourself with other guys, but do reply to a question about what you've been up to honestly or a photograph of you and your date doing something novel.

For instance, maybe you went to a wildlife sanctuary on your date and have an amusing image of an owl landing on your date's head. That's something worth posting – but a staged selfie of the two of you together in the bathroom mirror probably is not. The former is a comedy moment anyone might share. The latter looks as though you just want him to know you have a new man.

As he starts to notice you returning to normal and, horror of horrors, moving on without him, he will have no choice but to consider what that means for him. And because he is a man and naturally inclined to guard his possessions, he will feel all the jealousy and upset that you want him to feel.

After all, he's the one who dumped you. He might be moving on, and he won't think that's a strange thing to do, but it's going to be a body blow to see you doing the same. And by reminding him of this, you set the stage for making contact and, a little later down the road, reconciliation.

Step 8: Take a Reality Check

We're coming ever closer to the moment you've been waiting for: the moment when you are finally ready to make contact with your ex. But, before you do, you will need to take a reality check to make absolutely sure that you're ready for all that contact with your ex is going to entail.

As soon as you see him again, you're going to feel the same urges you felt right at the beginning. You're going to want to run to him and fling yourself into his arms, at least metaphorically speaking. This cannot happen if your plans are to be successful. You HAVE to make him work for you, or he isn't going to bother trying.

To a man, there are few things less attractive than a woman who is obviously needy and demands that her man be responsible for her happiness. He doesn't want you to cling to him and, if you do so now, he's going to rightfully assume it's indicative of how you'll act if he decides to take you back – and that's going to put him off instantly.

It's time to analyze your behavior as a girlfriend – your relationship personality. I want you to take a look at the list of behaviors below and ask yourself two questions about them. Is this how you would normally act in a relationship? And is it something that you're likely to do if the two of you get back together?

Answering yes to one of those questions doesn't mean answering yes to them both, of course. Ideally, you will say "no" to both of them. However, what we're hoping for here most of all is a definite "no" at least to the second question.

If you think it's something that's likely to happen, you're going to need to work through it before you get back in contact so you don't sabotage your chances of reconciling with your ex. Ask yourself why you do it and whether it's actually having a positive effect on you or on the relationship, under any circumstances at all.

Decide what measures you can take to stop yourself from doing it – and then make sure you follow through.

- You dislike it when he spends time with other people and doesn't invite you.
- You want to know exactly where he is at all times and who with.

- You text or call him when you're not together, but you don't really have anything you need to say.
- You think he's going to end things every time the two of you ague.
- You're passive aggressive when he doesn't show enough affection or attention.
- You put him ahead of absolutely everything else in your life, even important family commitments.

Think you act or are likely to act in any of those ways? Think again: you're going to need to drop these behaviors before you can get your ex back and be sure the relationship is going to work.

Step 9: Be Elusive

While you're doing all this work to better yourself and take a reality check on your mental and emotional status, it isn't uncommon for your ex to start trying to initiate contact. He may even have been doing so all along.

Why? Because, by now, you have successfully dumped all those feelings of rejection and lack of attention onto him. The way you were feeling at the beginning of this break up process is beginning to become his everyday experience.

We've been building up to this point all along. At first, he expected his phone to ring constantly and for it to be you on the other end, begging him to come back. He opened his email or messenger expecting great long missives of sorrow and distress.

He expected, in other words, to be the sole focus of your attention. And no matter how angry or displeased he was with you and the relationship, it hurt when that wasn't what he got.

From the moment you made it clear that you weren't just frozen in disbelief and this really was the way you planned to play things, he felt as though you abandoned him. It's this emotion, more than any other, that makes us question whether we really want a person to stop being in our life. And the answer is going to be: no.

This is because, meanwhile, you weren't crowding him with dramatics and continuing to dredge up all the negative feelings he had come to associate with the relationship. His abandonment forced him to think about you, and the complete removal of any mention of the bad side of the partnership forced him to think only about the positive aspects of you.

Now we're going to start adding in a third emotion: curiosity. We're going to dangle a little hope in front of him and then snatch it away again.

If he isn't already contacting you, it's fine to remind him of your presence, though this is another move you'll want to make with care. Contact him very briefly and without emotion for a genuine reason. Some good examples include:

- To return some of his personal items that he left at your house.
- To discuss financial arrangements as the two of you go your separate ways.

- To request information about bills, mortgage payments or anything else he usually handled but now falls to you.
- To remind him of an occasion you were responsible for arranging but he should still attend, such as a fundraiser that's important to him or because you have his e-tickets for a flight.

What do all these have in common? The fact that you are in no way suggesting the two of you get back together and are, in some cases, appearing to make a genuine step towards separating your lives. Never, ever even begin to suggest a reconciliation at this point.

So back to where we started in this chapter: he's now contacting you, often out of the blue. You're going to ignore most of those messages and calls and cherry pick the ones to respond to.

Give yourself a ball park figure to stick to, just to help you avoid giving in to temptation. For every message you do respond to, you're going to ignore the next three – at the very least. Five, if you can manage it.

When you do respond, the most important rule to follow is to always keep things light and cheerful. Avoid mentioning the break up (that comes later) and don't even joke about how badly you feel being without him. Not even a joke to the effect of, "Well if you hadn't smashed my heart into pieces, we wouldn't have to worry about the gas bill!" – all that's going to do is spark feelings of guilt or annoyance, and we don't want him thinking any negative thoughts at all about you right now.

When it feels appropriate, use inside jokes that only he will understand and references to happy times in your lives together. These things together will reinforce those positive feelings he's been having about you since you started to ignore him and the fact that you're starting to respond will give him a rush of hope.

And then, of course, you'll fail to respond to the next message, and then the next one. He'll drop back down into sadness and once again start pining for your attention, which will only engage his curiosity and determination to regain your affection even more.

He'll want to know why you're not responding, what you're doing that's so much more important than him and who you might be doing it with. He won't be able to resist that curiosity, so he'll have to resort to speaking with mutual friends or watching you on your social media accounts. Make no mistake: he will definitely be keeping a keen eye.

You're playing with his emotions here, yes, but it's a powerful tool for kick starting his heart. Whatever caused you to split up will have clouded out all the good things that caused you to fall in love. You're simply reminding him of them.

You won't be able to see any of this happening, so you'll have to stay strong and true and trust that, if he loved you and your relationship was once strong, it definitely will be happening.

Trust that all those primal instincts that make him want to win and conquer are now at play. You're not allowing him an easy win, so you're making him work all the harder, and there's nothing guys love more than a real challenge with a true prize at the end.

Step 10: Play on His Mind

Time to gather some momentum. You've piqued his curiosity and you've rekindled his desire to be near you, so let's step up our game to the next level. From here, the only way up is to make sure that he's thinking about you constantly.

We're going to play a few more little games that will have him wondering about you and wishing he was near you all day long.

You're going to start turning up in his life just when he least expects it. Unlike at first, when contacting him or appearing at his favorite bar would have seemed desperate, the beauty of doing so now is that he will not think of it as your way of begging him to come back. Instead, he will begin to anticipate those moments when you dart back into his life and right back out again and he will seek to make sure that they happen a whole lot more often.

We'll look at some ways to do that, but first a warning. You don't want to be doing this constantly and letting him see or hear from you three or four times a day. Start seldom and build up from there, making sure to maintain that air of mystery and unpredictability that got his interest back in your direction in the first place.

Never give him the impression he could have you back if he wanted you. Having given him the idea that you're a challenge worth trying for, your role now is to keep him at bay while his momentum builds up. Make him work for it – you've earned this moment.

So here are some ideas you might want to try, though obviously you'll want to adapt them to fit your circumstances:

- Get yourself invited to a party you know he'll be at, but make sure you don't stay all that long. Turn up with new friends if you can, just to make him wonder how you met them and who they are. Have fun and laugh, network all you can, say a polite and coquettish hello to him – and then leave. He'll stay behind, wondering what plans you had that were so much better than this party – and wondering what he could have done to be invited along with you.

- Send him a text message completely out of the blue. Something cheerful and humorous –

maybe you came across something that reminded you of a memory the two of you share or a joke that only he would really get. When he responds, leave it there – you're not eager to start a conversation, just sharing a thought with a friend, and that will drive him simply insane with curiosity.

- Run into him at a place you both frequent – it might take a little planning, but it's possible. Don't stay long and make sure to be on your happiest behavior. Try not to panic if he's with someone else, even if it's a woman. And if you can take a male friend along with you, so much the better, because he won't expect you, as the dumped party, to be moving on.

- Step up your participation in social media. Talk to his friends and mutual acquaintances in much the same way as I suggested in an earlier chapter, but with even greater focus on how well everything is going for you. Believe you me, he's going to see it, and he's going to wonder why it is you're so happy without him.

All the time you're doing this, you want to be reaffirming your agreement that the relationship is over. You can do this really quite subtly, simply by referring to the changes you've made in your life or by asking questions and making statements that imply you've moved on and want to make sure things are ended properly.

Ask him to return the movies you loaned him right at the beginning of your dating, the ones you so wanted him to watch because they show the landscape of the place you both wanted to go on vacation. Don't show any emotion – you simply want them back so you can watch them again.

Ask him if he knows where your passport is because "we" are planning a trip. He doesn't have to know where – and he doesn't need to know who "we" is.

Ask him for the details of your joint bank account so you can make sure that it's closed down and out of service.

You get the picture. Throw these in among the glimmers of hope you keep giving him to throw him off the scent and keep his emotions – and his curiosity and desire to win you back to him – completely out of whack.

Step 10: Avoid His Bait at All Costs!

For this next part to work, you'll need to understand on a deep and instinctive level what's going on in his head. To your ex boyfriend, you are a belonging.

I know that sounds insulting, but it's not meant to be. You belong to him just like his favorite jacket does, or his motorcycle. You are something that he thinks of as his to protect, spend time with and show off. If you think about it honestly, you count him among your belongings too.

The love between you belongs to him, and what you've done with all this work is make him question that. He may or may not be ready to admit to you – or even himself – that he's prepared to give your relationship another go, but you can bet your bottom dollar that he at least knows he wants his stuff back.

He's going to reach out to you at this point to test exactly where the relationship between you stands: this is the landmark moment you've been waiting for, and also the moment when you know that your hard work has paid off. But the time isn't quite right yet for you to accept his advances, so listen closely.

He's going to call you or text you, and he's going to ask you to get together with him. He'll likely phrase it very casually, suggesting you grab a quick dinner or meet for a chat.

You can choose either to say yes or no at this point, depending on how well you think your willpower is likely to hold out. If you think you'll be fine, agree to his request, with dignity and aloofness, and meet up with him – but make sure you treat him as you would any other friend and resist any attempts he makes to talk about "the two of you".

If you don't think you can make it through a whole meeting, just say no and make an excuse.

It doesn't actually matter either way because ultimately you'll be achieving the same effect: you'll be refusing to confirm for him that he isn't losing his possession.

There's no precise timeframe within which this will happen – it could take days or weeks, it might take months. Just know that, when it does happen – and believe me, it's going to – it's an important step for you and one at which you absolutely cannot stumble.

Again: do not give in to his temptation and do not take the bait! Leave him hanging, because it's only going to make him try even harder to win you back.

If you let him know how you're really feeling, he'll walk away content that he can have you whenever he wants to. If he walks away still completely unsure, he'll be stepping up his game before you know it.

Step 11: Have THAT Conversation

At this point, your ex boyfriend is going to be in constant contact with you – or, at least, he's going to be trying to be in constant contact. You're hearing from him all the time and things will start to progress from simple conversations and attempts to flirt. He's now making it very clear that he wants to try again.

Use your intuition – listen to it carefully. You'll see the change when it happens and you'll be able to tell that he's moved on from, "I want my stuff back" to, "Sweet lord, I think I threw away the best thing that ever happened to me".

Mark that change in your heart, because it means your time has come. And make no mistake: if you've been following my advice to the letter, your time IS going to come.

When you decide to accept his invitation and meet up with him to have the conversation you've been waiting for all along, it's important to make sure that you're doing so on your own terms – never his. Don't change your calendar to suit his suggestion: offer a time when you will be free and ready for what's coming. And don't accept his choice of venue, either, unless you really do love it. Show him that he is not in control of what's happening and that he's still going to need to put some effort in.

And above all else, be sure you're ready. Do you have your life all patched back up and better than ever? Have you accepted that you really are a prize worth winning? Are you able to think about this relationship with objectivity and are no longer breaking down in tears at the very mention of his name?

Good: that's exactly where you need to be. Now we need to show him that, so let's prepare ourselves. When he sees you, he needs to know right away that he's dealing with a new woman – one who may possibly be interested in what he has to say, but who definitely is not dependent on getting back together with him.

Wear your newest outfit, the one you feel absolutely gorgeous in. Spritz on a new and alluring perfume, do your hair in a way he's never seen. Have brand new conversation topics ready and waiting – your new hobbies, new friends and all the exciting things you've been getting up to. Make sure you've told him you can't stay long because you have obligations –

even ask a couple of friends to call you during that timeframe to show him how busy you are.

All of this tells him how much effort he's going to need to put in. Now you need only sit back and wait to see how he's going to approach this. Wait to let him speak, never bring the subject up first, and then listen to what he has to say very carefully.

- If he skirts around the subject, never quite telling you how he really feels but implying that he wants you to tell him what you want, don't answer directly. Make it clear that you're neither here nor there about the idea and that, if things are going to go back to how they were before, you will need to see some changes. Don't be negative or complain about how things were before. Instead, say something to the effect of, "Things are going really well for me right now and, if we are going to try things again, we need to look at how we're communicating our feelings with each other. If you aren't prepared to do that, I can look for someone who is."

- If he shows off about how brilliant his life is and how many things he's accomplished since you split up, don't fall for it. He's just acting like a peacock, trying to win you back. Wait for an opportune time and be frank: you've only got so much time for this conversation, so what does he want to talk to you about? If he doesn't back down, you may have misjudged the timing and it's better to back away and let him try again when he's ready for the challenge.

- If he's angry with you, listen out for jealousy. He's more likely to be irritated about how well you're moving on than still angry over what caused the two of you to break up. Again, don't rise to it. Again, demand with a perfectly straight face that he tell you what he wanted to speak with you about. If you still can't pin him down, tease him a little to make it plain you can see what he's doing.

- If he lays it all out on the table and asks you to come back to him, you've hit the jackpot. Having said that, it's still vital that you make sure he knows you hold the cards and that it's your choice whether to accept his offer or not. Make your thoughts known as to what has to change in your relationship and demand an answer as to whether he can provide what you need.

By the time this conversation ends, the two of you will have reached an understanding that you both want to try again but that there need to be some changes before you do. And you've also reached the understanding that you are choosing to let this happen and haven't been hanging around waiting for the call all this time.

Congratulations – you've done it! You've got your ex boyfriend back in your life and all you need to do now is be sure to build a new relationship that's stronger, better and more fulfilling than the one which fell apart.

What Happens if He's With Someone Else?

A lot of women I've worked with have tried to rush through the steps that I advocate, and it's always for the same reason. They're terrified that, if they leave things alone too long, their ex really will move on and find someone else to share their lives and bed with.

I want you to let go of that notion. There are only a few reasons for a guy to find a new girlfriend this quickly after a break up and most of them work in your favor:

- He was already with her – and if that's the case, you don't want to get back with the cheating bastard anyway. You can move on and forget him without worrying about any "what ifs" and "if onlys".

- He was lonely – in which case, it's not really her he's interested in and he's not going to choose her over you. What he misses is the intimacy he had with the woman he really loves.

- He felt like he should – it's very common, and it even has a name: rebound relationships. Fortunately for you, the vast majority of these crumble very quickly.

No matter his reasons, he's not going to be as comfortable in this new relationship as he was with you – she is just a distraction. If he's truly going to come back to you, it won't matter.

It will make it harder for you, I accept that fact – and so must you. You'll want to stalk him on social media to check for signs that he's happier with her than he was with you. You'll want to compare yourself to her in every way possible. You'll hurt like hell every time you think of the two of them together.

But it doesn't change what you have to do and it has no real impact on your chances. Do not – I repeat, do NOT – try to hurry things along just in case he falls more deeply in love with her while you're dithering. Remember that every single step you take draws him just that little bit closer to you… and a little bit further from her.

And if you see the two of them together out in public? Hide that pain, no matter how hard it stabs you in the chest. Think of this as an opportunity: you get to show him how far you really have moved on because you're honestly not fussed what he's getting up to. Even though you feel betrayed, like a lesser woman, hurt and hopeless, never show it. And never underestimate the impact that reaction is going to have on him.

The mantra to hold in your head and your heart if you discover he's hooked up with another girl is: it doesn't change your plan. You are still going to win him back.

A Final Word: Building a Better, Stronger Future With Your Ex

You might think the journey is over now that your man is back in your arms again and all is just right with the world. You've reached your goal and your heart is once again whole.

I'm thrilled for you, I honestly am – how you're feeling right now is exactly the reason that I wrote this book in the first place. I wanted you to be able to win back the love that hurt so much when it was torn away.

But I also want to turn your attention back to the beginning of this book. There's a reason that the two of you broke up, and simply getting back together probably isn't enough to solve that problem.

Now you've won him back, your journey really begins. This was more than just a bump in the road: this was your chance to step back, reevaluate what the two of you had and what was missing and then do whatever it takes to fix it.

To do that takes work – a whole lot of work in fact. But it's going to be worth it. I'm going to finish up this book by giving you a few pointers to get you started. It's really the final step in getting back together, rather than the first step of building your brand new life together. It's just as necessary as every other step I had you take throughout this book.

And if you're secretly planning to put down the book and get on with being happy, just remember this: I haven't steered you wrong so far, have I?

No, I haven't, so trust me for just a little bit longer. Follow these final steps and you're guaranteed to keep hold of that love you've just won back – now, and into your future.

- **Don't bottle up your emotions.** You're bound to have a lot of residual anger, fear, hurt and betrayal – of course you are. The two of you broke up and it left you with a shattered heart. None of that has simply dissolved and disappeared. Nor will you be alone in this: he will have a whole lot of negative emotions still swimming around too, and the two of you need to resolve them. So let them out, but do so in a controlled manner. Set a time aside for the two of you to talk it out and agree beforehand that you can scream, shout and throw things to your heart's desire. This is nothing more than a purge: a moment to get all of those feelings out and say the things you need to say. No matter what comes out of it, agree to understand that the past is the past and this is just the final dregs of it. Give each other permission to go completely crazy, if you need to.

- Listen to the reasons you split up. Whatever it was that happened, you need to talk about it. This is best done after you've had your agreed upon screaming match, of course. You don't want to fall into the same traps again and you want to understand each other. However painful you think it is going to be, it's important that you sit down and listen to each other and be completely honest about what caused the problem. Did one of you cheat or betray the other in some way? Both of you need to understand why. The culprit needs to admit why and get that off their chest, and the one who got hurt needs to hear it. And then, you need to learn from it and let it go.

- Agree to let the past be the past. Both of you need to do this or it won't work. Whatever happened in your previous relationship had to do with exactly that – your *previous* relationship. This is not the same partnership.

It's a fresh start with a clean slate and you'll only make a proper go of it if you can leave all those slights and hurts and betrayals in the past. Don't leave this one to chance. Instead, you should pledge it to one another out loud. He may never think to do that, so take it upon yourself to approach the subject. Let him know you never want the bad things to happen again, but you also don't want to constantly dwell on them. Ask him to pledge with you that the past is the past and you both have the right to shut down any arguments, recriminations or allusions to anything that happened before you split up. This one, of course, can only happen once you've resolved all of those issues between the two of you.

- Communicate like you have never communicated before. This one can be hard, if you're a private sort of person who doesn't like to wear their heart on their sleeve. It's also the lifeblood of the relationship you're hoping to build. As you move forward, you need to be able to talk about anything that's going wrong, especially if it reminds you of what went wrong before. You need to remember that you are now working as a team to solve the same problem and reach the same goal – that goal being happiness and a strong relationship. Team mates do not work alone. No matter how hard it is to broach a subject, how embarrassed you feel or that you think you might be making a mountain out of a mole hill, it's something you have to do. Constantly, until it becomes second nature.

- **Figure out what was missing.** This is slightly different to talking through the exact problem that caused your split. Instead, it's about working out why it was that one or both of you were not satisfied with your relationship, which is likely the underlying cause of the problems you were having. For instance, let's say he dumped you because he'd had enough of the two of you fighting all the time. But why were you fighting? Maybe it was because you were feeling neglected and because he wasn't spending enough time with you, so you provoked him to get that attention. In that case, what was missing was quality time together. Promise each other that you will do everything in your power to fill those gaps, because that will complete your relationship and guarantee that both of you stay happy with it.

- **Make some changes.** Why go back to normal when you can go back to something even better? Even if the two of you were together for a couple of decades, you haven't tried every new experience there is, nor done every romantic thing there is to do for one another. A new start is a new beginning in more than one way. It's time to bring back all that romance and heady joy from the early days and make sure that it lasts. All that work you did to improve your own life? It's time to let him in on it too. Include him in your new hobbies and social circles and get involved in the things that he loves to do too. It doesn't matter if these things don't instantly appeal – you don't have to try it again if you don't like it, but you'll still have had a new adventure together. Turn this relationship into a rollercoaster of excitement and laughter – trust me, you'll never for a second regret it.

So here we are, right at the end: exactly where I promised you would be. You have your ex boyfriend back – actually, we can stop calling him your ex altogether. He is now simply your boyfriend, your partner and your team mate.

Enjoy the fruits of all that labor – you earned this happiness many times over. What you did to get to this point was not easy, I've seen a lot of women stumble over and over along the way.

But you did it. You stayed strong and true and you got your man back, and I'm so proud of you for doing it. With a smile on my face, I'll step back and leave you to enjoy every moment of your reconciliation. Every kiss you longed for all this time, every part of your lifestyle that you shared and couldn't wait to share again.

Congratulations, my friend. You've conquered the game of love – you got your ex boyfriend back.

Made in the USA
Monee, IL
19 February 2020